IF SELECTIVE MUTISM HAD A VOICE;

A TRUE AND COMPELLING STORY ABOUT MY STRUGGLE WITH A SEVERE ANXIETY DISORDER AND HOW I OVERCAME IT THROUGH CHRISTIAN FAITH PRINCIPLES AND PRACTICAL TECHNIQUES

DANIELA PARLANE

Copyright © 2018 by Daniela Parlane.

WHY I WROTE THIS BOOK

I wrote this book because I have a passion for helping others by providing them with the tools I gained through life experience and digging into God's Word on how to overcome the paralyzing anxiety disorder of Selective Mutism.

DEDICATION

I dedicate this book to my amazing mother, Maria, who never stopped believing in me, supporting me and loving me throughout all the difficult moments in my life. I owe her a lot of credit for the progress I've made over the years and ultimately defeating the crippling disorder of Selective Mutism.

Table of Contents

CHAPTER 1 KINDERGARTEN: 1986-1987	6
FROZEN	6
RECESS	8
CHAPTER 2	9
FORK IN THE ROAD	10
CURIOSITY IS HUMAN NATURE, BUT NOT ALWAYS HUMANE	11
MISUNDERSTOOD	12
CHAPTER 3 IN RETROSPECT	15
ADVICE	15
CAUSE?	16
CHAPTER 4 LIFE BEFORE SELECTIVE MUTISM	18
CHAPTER 5 GRADE 1: 1987-1988	20
"KARATE CHOPS"	21
SET BACKS	22
RECITAL	23
CHAPTER 6 ELEMENTARY SCHOOL: 1987-1992	26
OBSTACLE COURSE	26
CHAPTER 7	31
CHURCH LIFE	31
OUT AND ABOUT	32
SET APART	32
CHAPTER 8	34
SENSORY PROCESSING ISSUES	34
"STIMMING" BEHAVIOURS	34
CHAPTER 9 GROWING PAINS	38
CHAPTER 10 MULTIPLE PERSONALITIES?	38
CHAPTER 11 MIDDLE SCHOOL: 1992-1995	42
MILESTONES	43
'COMPLEX' SITUATIONS	44

CHAPTER 12 HIGH SCHOOL: 1995-1999	45
GETTING GROUNDED	46
CHAPTER 13	49
ADULTHOOD: BLOSSOMING	50
TODAY'S PROGNOSIS	51
THE STRUGGLES: ANXIETY	53
SENSORY PROCESSING ISSUES	55
"STIMS"	56
CHAPTER 14 CONFIDENCE TIPS	57
TAKE THE BULL BY THE HORNS	59
CHAPTER 15	64
SAY NO TO PHARMACEUTICAL DRUGS	64
DIETARY TIPS	66
CHAPTER 16 LIGHT AT THE END OF THE TUNNEL	67
CHAPTER 17 EMBRACE YOUR QUIRKS	70

CHAPTER 1
Kindergarten: 1986-1987

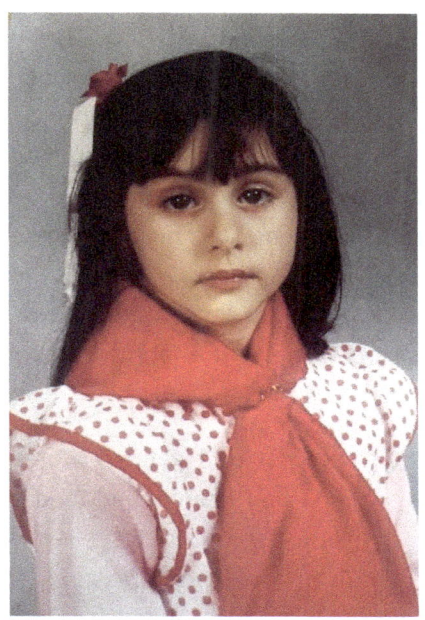

FROZEN

I held my mom's hand with a grip of death, as I felt the heat radiating off my clenched, sweaty palms. An eerie sensation swept over my gut as I took the first step into a whole new world—the world that I would soon know as kindergarten. The smell of crayons hung in the air. Alphabet letters lined the chalkboard; neatly stacked colorful bins filled the shelves. Building blocks, puzzles, and books galore, with a painting station, a sandbox, and even a piano. It all lured me in like a worm on a hook—but somehow, I couldn't shake the foreboding queasiness in my gut. Then it happened—children—*alien* children—were everywhere. These children didn't seem like the ones I was familiar with. I didn't know them. They were so strange to me. This place—so large, colorful and happy felt like more of a kiddie-trap, kind of like Pleasure Island from the Pinocchio story. A wave of paralysis took over my body. I couldn't speak— I felt stiff, uncomfortable and afraid—and I couldn't understand why. What was wrong with me? I couldn't explain my reaction to this new atmosphere. Everyone was so cheerful, especially my kindergarten teacher. But it seemed that the more people approached me, the more I wanted to crawl into a corner and hide. My mom prompted me to say "hi" to my newfound acquaintances, but the more I tried to force my voice out of my throat, the more it closed up and I completely froze. My heart was beating a mile a minute. It felt as though my vocal cords had shut down. I couldn't make sense of it, and I was so afraid. My entire reality shifted into a swirl of abyss and fear snowballed into a vicious cycle at the fact that I didn't know why I was so afraid in the first place.

Just when I thought things couldn't get any worse, my mom left the room—and I felt as though I had been abandoned in the shadow of the valley of death. I was like a fish out of water—I wanted to cry, but I couldn't. But then an air of conviction pressed me to be strong. I had decided that nobody here was ever going to see my emotions. My only option was asserting myself that I was going to make it through the next moment. At least this area was something I could control, and I did an exceptional job at that. In a world where I felt insecure and afraid, I had instinctually found some way to cope by overcompensating in self-composure.

The questions soon came at me like fiery darts. I just wanted them to stop!

"Why don't you speak?"
"Just say one word"
"Hellooo are you there?"
"Are you normal?"
"Can you hear me?"

"Are you dumb?"
"If you can hear me, how many fingers am I holding up?"
"She doesn't speak"
"She's weird"
"Just leave her alone, she doesn't say anything"

Their voices echoed in my mind as I would look away with a blank stare. I could feel my cheeks flushing as I tried to hide behind my long dark hair. Whispers, murmurs and giggles ensued. I looked down at my hands and picked the skin around my nails. I would bite my upper lip, and find some way to keep myself busy and out of the spotlight. I couldn't help but ponder upon how drastically different I was outside of this room. Sadly, the more the days went by, the more I felt the impending doom unravel its fury upon me.

RECESS

The recess bell rang, and the children raced for the door. Everyone was excited about which monkey bars they were going to swing on, or the sand box they were going to shovel in. For me it was always the same old story. I was the little girl who sat and played alone in the corner. On this particular day, I was faced with a new horrifying reality. Ironically, for any other child, this would have been a reason for great happiness and excitement; for me, it meant the possible loss of someone important. Who did I see sitting in the sandbox that day? It was none other than my best friend who lived down my street. I scanned the area as the terrifying reality sunk in. Other children were everywhere. I couldn't speak! She had no idea about my 'problem'. Her freckled face lit up instantly as she ran over to me, jumping and laughing. I was even ashamed to look into her crystal blue squinty eyes. She crumpled her freckled nose in confusion. To her shock and disappointment, I couldn't bring myself to utter a word. I just stared at her paralyzed, wishing my saddened eyes would somehow transmit what I was experiencing. But the more she raised the pitch of her voice expecting a response, the more I froze with a void expression on my face. The seconds felt eternal, and I wanted to sink into a hole and bury myself deep into the earth. I was ashamed, yet I couldn't explain this phenomenon. I was terrified that I had possibly just lost my best friend, by simply not being able to speak. I would lose the ability to open my mouth as soon as *they* were around. It was unfamiliar territory, as if someone had plucked me out of my habitat, and dropped me in a den of hyenas. It was indescribable. My best friend was hurt, and I hurt for her in return as I watched her stomp away in disgust. Her strawberry blond locks bounced behind her in indignation. I felt the formation of tears at the rim of my eyes, but quickly swallowed back my pain, as I choked back my tears and turned away.

I was elated and relieved at the fact that she later gave me the opportunity to explain to the best of my ability, what had happened at school. Yet the 'situation' was simply labeled as "I can't talk when I'm at school". Despite the strangeness of this phenomenon, she forgave me and accepted me for the way I was. I was grateful to have her in my life. As fortunate as I was for the way things panned out, things didn't always work out so well.

CHAPTER 2

FORK IN THE ROAD

Fun filled the air as I ran around carelessly in the field, playing tag with my little cousin. Shortly after, we opted to play on the swing-set at the park down the street. Almost immediately, two very friendly brunettes approached us. Being with my cousin was so natural to me, and playing in my neighborhood was completely comfortable and familiar. It was home. It wasn't long before the new girls mingled with us as if we'd known each other for years. We played together and took turns pushing each other on the swings. It was just another ordinary happy day for me—until a few days later.

It was on one bright summer's day that my entire school convened with the school across the street for some type of end-of-year summer play event—and who spotted me in the crowd? You guessed it, the brunettes. I froze as our eyes met, and tried my hardest to lose eye contact, and play it off as if I hadn't noticed them. If only I could diverge their attention elsewhere. If only I could pretend that I didn't see them, and spare this enormously panicky feeling of heaviness pressing on my chest. My heart started racing, and my face went hot. The palms of my hands got all clammy, and I lost all focus on what was going on around me. Everything felt as though it was in 'slow motion'. Every step they took closer towards me, my heart would pound harder and dizziness would sweep over me; but this time, I couldn't avoid the moment of bitter truth, the inevitable impending horror, when they would approach me giddily, only to be reciprocated by total and absolute unresponsiveness. It's no surprise what happened next; the one girl made sure I heard her flippantly tell the other "I guess we should not bother speaking to Daniela again, since she doesn't want to be our friend anymore". Every word that dropped out of her lips fell on my heart like burning daggers. I wanted to shout after them and ask them to stay, and that I was still their friend. I wanted to tell them I don't talk at school; but I couldn't, and it was already too late. My lips were sealed, and my heart was broken. The crude reality that foreshadowed me was fulfilled, and the girls never spoke to me again.

CURIOSITY IS HUMAN NATURE, BUT NOT ALWAYS HUMANE...

My entire life had drastically changed in such a short time, and yet it wasn't about to stay the same. Naively, I had no idea what cruelties lied ahead, and I had stepped into a den of lions with my own two feet. Who knew children could be so cruel, by simply turning off your speech? Well, I was about to find out soon enough. Kids would bully and tease me and even physically abuse and ridicule me, in attempts to get a sound out of me—or simply because they were fully aware that there would be no consequences to follow. This all spurred from their curiosity. Why wasn't this girl like all the other kids? What would she do if I pulled her hair, or pinched her really hard? Would she cry or make a sound? Would she suddenly start to speak? To their great discovery, this only clamped me up more. I had officially turned into the class freak. *The weirdo. The mute.* Children would pinch, punch, kick, push and scratch me and pull my hair in a curiously sadistic attempt to hear me make a sound in my defense. It perpetuated a vicious cycle—the more they would harm me, the more I withdrew. I was determined to endure the pain at all costs, so long as my voice wasn't heard.

I vividly remember the dreaded story time in kindergarten class—every single day, the same pudgy blond-haired mean girl would sit right next to me on the rug. She would feign affection towards me, when in actuality, she was scheming to secretly grab a chunk of the skin on my upper thigh, and twist it to the point of instant bruising; her ruddy complexion would change to a bright red hue as she giggled in devilish delight each time she did it—and yet I never once gave her the satisfaction of making a peep. My tolerance only grew, and I viewed any response to pain or cry for help as weakness. I avoided this at any cost.

Another day, I was so elated from having received a balloon from my kindergarten teacher, just as it was time to pack up and get ready to go home. I was exuberant with excitement as I walked to my cubby, when one little boy came and deliberately grabbed the balloon from my grip, popped it, laughed, and smugly handed me the rubber shredded remains. Perhaps he sensed my glee. Perhaps I had allowed myself to crack a smile—just once. I was instantly overcome with pain and great shame for allowing myself those few minutes of innocent bliss. At that very tender age of five, tightness gripped my throat as I resisted the urge to cry. I straightened up, chin up, and continued slipping on my gloves and toque as if nothing had transpired. Needless to say, that day I shut down even more.

MISUNDERSTOOD

Another horrible disadvantage of not speaking was the huge margin of misinterpretation of my actions, by teachers especially. On one particularly dreadful day, the teacher had asked everyone to 'tidy up' and put all of the toys away. I was playing with building blocks, and decided to sort them in an organized fashion before putting them into their designated box. The teacher must have construed this as defiance, thinking that I had ignored her instructions and continued to play. She got very upset with me and told me to go straight to the office. I was immensely shocked and saddened by her behavior, especially since the teacher was usually very patient and kind towards me. I had never gotten in trouble before. I was always very compliant.

The office was a whole other category of doom in itself. The principal was notoriously feared for her less than kind conduct with the children. She was short, round and stubby, with really short dark hair, and the temper of a savage beast. She always wore the same dull, brown 'principle suit'. We would hear her squealing voice ricocheting down the school hallways on a regular basis, as she tore her victims apart, in the confinement of her cold and creepy little office.

My kindergarten teacher preceded my steps as I gloomily made my way to the office. She marched ahead of me into the office and started her complaint against me—her version of the event anyways. Panic took over my body as I felt hot tears starting to form behind my eyelids. I did everything in my power to hold them back. As I sunk back in the hard, wooden chair, the principle proceeded in bombarding me with questions. Her raspy voice grew louder and more punctuated. Her efforts were futile, as all I could do was stare blankly back at her, then look away with glossy eyes. Then, she hit a really weak spot—she threatened to call my mother. Total dread swept over me as I held back my tears and I started to sob uncontrollably—inwardly, in silence. I choked back every sob, but it became progressively difficult. I had to stay strong. I had to keep it together. Her threats were to no avail, so she didn't waste any more time; she furled her bushy brows at me, and she stretched her stubby fingers towards the phone.

CHAPTER 3
In Retrospect

ADVICE

If there's one very valuable piece of advice I could share with parents, as well as guardians, teachers or anyone else involved in a child's life with Selective Mutism it's this: the worst thing you can do is pressure and attempt to force a child or threaten them in order to get them to speak! This will only make matters worse, and my parents understood that very quickly—it was a learning process for them despite their frustration.

My older brother and I were a relatively novel case, according to a speech pathologist that told my parents that their children were the first cases of this disorder he had heard of in 30 years; consequently, it was extremely difficult to diagnose. Selective Mutism wasn't easily recognized and/or properly diagnosed until more recent years. At the time, it was considered rare and was known as 'Elective Mutism' suggesting the child makes a liberal *choice* not to speak out of *defiance*—two premises which are totally false. It was only in recent years that it was acknowledged to be a social *anxiety* disorder which actually renders the child *unable* to speak. Upon further investigations, thus the term for this disorder was changed to 'Selective Mutism' in 1994.

In retrospect, I would advise parents of especially younger children with SM to consider homeschooling if possible. I am convinced that had my parents taken this route, I would have transitioned into society much more smoothly, and at my own pace. Understandably, this may not be a viable option for everyone; consider making arrangements to volunteer at school or places where the child is mute. I believe this would have tremendously eased my anxiety and allowed me to feel more familiar with my surroundings. Also, perhaps try arranging a playdate in your home with another parent of a child in the class. Another option is to speak to parents of other children and coordinate extra-curricular activities such as swimming, art, dance classes, park or library visits. The premise is to create familiar environments so the child can gradually ease into their formerly foreign environment.

Cause

Lindsay Whittington, co-ordinator and founding member of the Selective Mutism Information and Research Association (SMIRA) says: "While it's thought to affect approximately 1 in every 150 children, Selective Mutism (SM) is relatively unheard of. No single cause of selective mutism has been established, though emotional, psychological and social factors may influence its development. In the past these children were thought to be manipulative or angry, but research now points strongly to social anxiety, similar to 'stage fright'.

"Some of the signs or symptoms of selective mutism may include: an inability to make eye contact; nervousness; social awkwardness; an inability to initiate conversations; and a frozen and expressionless appearance during the periods of mutism. Some children with SM may also appear stubborn, but this is borne out of their need to control their anxiety levels, and some have a tendency to periods of aggression or tantrums in the home due to personal frustrations."

I could practically have been a poster child for this disorder, exempting the listed aggression and tantrums. I was the opposite in that regard and just internalized my emotions, even at home.

As noted in an excerpt by Dr. E. Steven Dummit, Advisory Board Member of The Selective Mutism Foundation:

"The child is just being stubborn and controlling by not talking." This belief is so pervasive that the disorder was called "Elective Mutism" for over 50 years, as if these children made a conscious decision, or "elected" at some point, to quit talking. It is assumed that such "controlling" behavior is a result of conflicts in the parent-child relationship, with the child attempting to win the struggle by resorting to mutism. In this view of the problem, parents, usually the mother, are assumed to lack parenting skills, or character strength or such, and are thus blamed for the child's disorder. Fortunately, modern child psychiatry is moving away from such outmoded theories. Most of the reports of Selective Mutism published in the past decade recognize the disorder as stemming from severe social anxiety and excessive inhibition, not from bad parenting."

As was initially suspected of my parents, this disorder was formerly speculated to derive from domestic abuse and neglect, due to the limited information that was available about Selective Mutism in the 80's. Due to this erroneous thinking, my parents were put under the microscope as a result. Much investigation ensued. They were inspected by a Children's Aid nurse who spent three hours a day for an entire week to observe our behavior as a family unit and to thoroughly investigate our living conditions before ruling out any form of domestic abuse in the household. After much examining us with a fine tooth comb, the nurse found absolutely no domestic issues and even commended my mother, who was a stay-at-home mother at the time, for her excellent parenting skills. Nutritious meals were always cooked from scratch. My mother spent most of her time engaging in fun and educational activities with us. Discipline was carried out within reason and in love. There was no lack of affection where we were concerned.

Needless to say, this journey was an emotional roller-coaster for my family and a learning experience for everyone involved; my siblings and I, our parents, doctors and educational staff.

CHAPTER 4

LIFE BEFORE SELECTIVE MUTISM

Let's rewind. I was born in June of 1981 and lived in a traditional family structure—and was the middle sibling of two brothers (born in 1979 and 1985). My parents are Italian immigrants and communicated with us in their mother tongue. Consequently, Italian was my first language. The three of us learned English mainly on our own—through television and friendships we had made living in our neighborhood. (Interestingly enough, although research studies on

SM are scarce, and despite the lack of research studies conducted, there has been a significant repeated pattern of SM children of bilingual backgrounds.)

By the time I started kindergarten, I spoke fluent English and language barrier was never a deterrent, although I admit that my knowledge of another tongue did at times contribute to my insecurities about speaking. I can relate to times when I was overwhelmed by a feeling of isolation due to the fact that this other language set me apart from my peers.

I was generally a shy child around strangers, but to the extent that one would consider normal or even common. I have no recollection of ever having SM before starting school. I had many friends on my block; we had playdates at the park, we hung out together in small and larger groups, I had birthday parties and attended friends' birthday parties. It was life as usual.

Back-tracking again—it is important to note, however, that my older brother had Selective Mutism. It all began when he started kindergarten as well. Things were tougher for him due to the fact that the school was totally in the dark about his condition. Consequently, he failed the first grade. They thought that his refrain from speaking was out of defiance. To make matters worse, they were unable to evaluate his progress as a result and decided it would be best for him to repeat the year. Our family moved shortly thereafter, and he was switched to another school. It was during this time that he was wrongly diagnosed with what was then still known as 'Elective Mutism', but it was a step forward and everyone did what they could with the limited knowledge that was available to them at the time. Some form of diagnosis was finally acknowledged, and a special program was put in place to aid him through his learning and eventual speaking.

After seeking counsel from a speech and language pathologist, my parents were told to stay on alert for when I would begin school. To their dismay, they had their work cut out for them with Selective Mutism child number two—followed by Selective Mutism child number three—my little brother.

What are the odds?

Chapter 5

Grade 1: 1987-1988

"Karate Chops"

I can still remember the smell of crayons and home-made glue, as I engaged in creative activities. That was one thing I was never afraid to do. I demonstrated a strong artistic inclination from a young age. As the ongoing Selective Mutism investigation continued among the family physician, pediatrician, speech pathologist, teachers and my parents, I took baby steps towards my recovery. I began by nodding, yes or no or shrugging my shoulders as if to say, "I don't know".

The middle to end of first grade was when I experienced my first verbal victory—the day I finally whispered in my teacher's ear for the first time. Of course, praise would only put me on the spot and slow down my progression, but discovering Selective Mutism was an experience not only for myself, but everyone around me. It wasn't long before I began to whisper in other children's ears— and I clearly remember uttering my first words "karate chops". Good humor and encouragement from teachers and peers served as a precursor in my recovery, despite the fact that too much attention was a recipe for immediate and total silence. There was a fine line to work in between. I was on a journey of my own, as I tried to discover myself, while those around me also tried to understand what I was going through, and why. That day marked an important milestone for me, and it was going to be a long, uphill trek to overcoming social anxiety. It wasn't going to be easy, but every tiny step graduated me into the right direction. My next words after "karate chops" were usually responses with yes or no. As I began to gradually progress, I would roll my eyes around as if searching for an answer (to buy time) and began to whisper short answers.

The system that proved very effective in my case is known today as "sliding in technique". It involves breaking down speaking activities into small manageable steps starting with a step that the child feels comfortable doing.

As the novelty of whispering began to wear off, I gradually began to speak 'out loud'.

SET-BACKS

With every victory, a setback was soon to follow.

I had begun to finally make friendships at school. I was progressing with speaking and even had girls asking me to walk home with me every night. They shared their snacks with me, and we played together at recess. One day, I was so thrilled when I was invited to one girl's house to play. I felt like a normal child. We laughed, played and had so much fun together. There was a moment where I almost couldn't believe it. I was normal. I had the ability to speak and to be liked. As exuberant as I was in my unabashed moment, it was rather short lived. Things took a turn for the worse when her mother suddenly stormed into the room and spoke to me in a very sharp voice asking:

"Where did you learn to say that?" I have no recollection of what I had said that could have been so alarming. I just remember innocently chasing after my friend and laughing together moments prior. I froze in fear as she continued to raise her voice at me. I couldn't speak and I felt my throat tightening. I had no idea what she was talking about, and I don't believe my friend did either. I was swiftly sent home and was told I was no longer welcome there. My heart sank to my socks.

The next day, my entire life changed. My friend no longer smiled at me. The play dates ended. She was no longer "allowed" to be my friend. Neither were her friends, according to her. Needless to say, I was broken. I didn't understand what had happened. My world at school quickly fell apart as I became the victim of suspicious stares, chuckles and murmuring. No more company walking home after school. No more recess friends. Goodbye to every crumb of joy I had worked so hard to achieve.

Recital

When I was about 7 years old, I was given a small part to recite in a church Christmas play. By this time, I had slowly begun coming out of my shell. I took small steps in talking within small groups that I felt I could trust. I had rehearsed my part many times in Sunday school class, but the day we had to recite in front of the church, everything changed. The church was exceptionally crowded that evening. All eyes were on me, it seemed. Camera flashes swept the crowd, and cheers reverberated throughout the building. Each child effortlessly spoke their part. Terror struck me harder at the thought that my turn was coming up. I felt like a sheep being led to the slaughter. It was my turn. Everything was deafeningly silent. Everything went into slow-motion. I froze. My lips couldn't move, and my throat felt tight. Eyes glazed over as I looked past the crowd. At one moment, I looked into my mother's eyes, and I wanted to cry. My thoughts castigated me with the idea that I would disappoint her yet again. She had waited so long for this moment, I thought to myself, when her daughter would be just like all the other children. She would finally perform and make her proud. But it all came to a halt. Guilt suffocated me, and I just wanted her to rescue me. She just looked at me, with eyes of admiration, and an encouraging smile on her face. But I would only respond with more silence. The Sunday school teacher prompted me gently by whispering my line in my ear as she held the microphone to my mouth—total deer-in-headlights look paralyzed my face—and the photograph lives on to prove it. The glassy- eyed, frozen still little angel in white, donning a sparkly halo that sat on top of the long black hair I tried to hide behind. Every imaginable complex came to mind in that never-ending moment; my big nose, strange looking ears, weird facial expression. It was like every part of me was being put under a giant microscope and keenly scrutinized by the crowd; the way I awkwardly moved my stiffened body. My fidgety footing. The way my lips quivered as I nervously bit my upper lip. The obvious blush of hot blood that flushed my olive-tinted cheeks. The fleeting eye movements I made to skillfully avoid eye-contact. I picked the skin around my nails and bit it off until my fingers looked like dried up prunes. It was one of my only coping mechanisms for terrifying situations such as these. The eternal moment of humiliation came and went, and I had failed miserably.

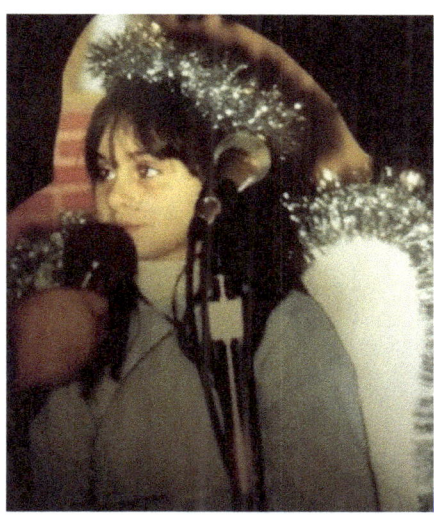

I was incredibly disappointed and angry at myself. I had determined within myself that I was going to recite my part. I was so proud of how far I had come, and that I too would finally be able to contribute towards a team effort. I was going to make my parents proud—but I blew it.

I allowed obsessive fearful thoughts to steal my opportunity. That day, I emotionally regressed back into my dark silent past.

Chapter 6

Elementary School: 1987-1992

Obstacle Course

As I embarked on a novel journey to pre-pubescence, there were new challenges that I was going to have to face. Even as I grew older, from grades one to five, there were times when boys especially would wait for me after school to 'teach me a lesson'. Fortunately for me, I can say I made up for my speech impediment with physical strength. Their feeble attempts to beat the words out of me backfired when they'd get kicked back or I'd fiercely block their blows. I have some Jackie Chan in me, what can I say? Had I not physically defended myself, matters would have been much worse. These experiences caused my condition to waver. In a sense, I would get stronger and more confident in my physical and inner strength—but on another level, I would resort to verbally shutting down that much more, at the constant reminder that I was different. A weirdo. A freak.

When the bullying and abuse happened, I didn't always tell my mom. I had learned to live with it most times, mainly because I was so afraid of confrontation. There were few times when I eventually told my mom about repeat offenders, but was afraid of what she would do. She found an effective method of dealing with the situation without causing me added anxiety: she would come to the school and ask me to point out the child. She would then give them a long, stern look with one raised eyebrow and speak loudly enough so that they could hear her say "Oh, is that the child that has been bothering you Daniela?" It always amazed me how swiftly they would stop bothering me after that. Nobody could withstand her look of death.

How could I forget that horrible day in grade two, when the mean tom-boy girl blocked me into the girl's bathroom and held me 'hostage' until I would 'cry'? No matter how badly I wanted to scream, cry, speak or merely respond, I would become overwhelmed with anxiety and fear which would result in emotional paralysis. On her receiving end—only a blank, expressionless glare, peering aimlessly around the stalls. That particular day, I was merely saved by a group of classmates who unknowingly interrupted this abuse, with their boisterous entrance.

I exhaled another temporary sigh of relief. But it was only a matter of time before I'd fall victim to someone else.

Regardless of my slow and gradual progress, the abuse didn't completely stop as I got older, and by this point I had become notoriously known at school for being super shy and 'different'. The more I was labeled, the more my progress would come to a halt. I felt obligated to live within the confines of that title. The simple act of pointing out my 'problem' or the fact that I was 'different' or 'shy' would increase my anxiety and immediately put me in 'shut down' mode. I kept my clothing as moderate and boring as possible. My hair was generally in the same style. I didn't like making changes that could be too noticeable, as it would add on to my complexes as well as draw too much attention.

The uphill battle continued. In grade 3, I had an encounter in the girl's bathroom yet again, with another girl who found great pleasure in mocking me. It was the same girl who befriended me in grade two and was no longer allowed to be my friend.
That day she observed me in the bathroom as I fixed a stray hair in the mirror's reflection. She looked at me with disgusted indignation; her crystal blue eyes were ice cold daggers. Who knew such a frail and innocent looking child could be so hateful? I suppose this behaviour came naturally to the popular spoiled kids. She was the pretty little blond girl who wore all the preppy clothes and hung around all the other popular trendy girls. I wondered whether her mother wanted to keep it that way. Perhaps nerdy girls like me weren't up to par with her standards.
Interestingly enough, this was the same ultra-sensitive girl who cried over the most trivial things, almost on a daily basis. You could just breathe the wrong way and streams would flow down her face. She was used to a huddle of friends swarming her with comfort each time she shed a tear. Your classic spoiled rotten child in constant need of attention. She always had a shoulder to cry on—however with me, she showed no such mercy. Not even a scrap.
She proceeded to ask me in the presence of her posse "let me guess, your mom tells you you're pretty, right? Does she tell you that?"
Her question prompted a feeble whispered "Yes"—then she went for the premeditated kill:
"Well she's the only person who thinks that—oh, and well let me guess, does she tell you someone will actually marry you one day?"

I felt totally ridiculed and humiliated, so I refrained from further responding. This only prompted her to proceed with "Well you better get used to the idea that nobody will ever want you".
Her voice trailed off in a prepubescent squeal. After a long awkward pause, she spun her stringy blond-haired head around and jubilantly frolicked away. Her friends followed her—their mocking giggles echoing along, imprinting on my mind— as they bore a hole into the mustard seed of hope for progress in overcoming SM. I picked up the remaining shreds of my bruised self-esteem and walked back to class as if nothing had happened.

When I was in grade five, there was one scenario in particular that really hit me like a ton of bricks—in fact, it hurt me more than the bullying I endured daily; that had become predictable and I was able to cope with it.
One time, a new girl was introduced to our class. She seemed very friendly and wanted to get to know me. That day, I overheard a conversation between her and another girl in my class, who I had considered one of my closer acquaintances because she treated me very kindly. I was privy to this exchange, unbeknownst to them.

The new girl asked discreetly: "Should I be friends with Daniela? She seems very nice"
To which the other girl I knew responded: "Oh her, she doesn't really talk very much. She's really weird. I only pretend to be her friend, but I don't actually like her. Nobody does".

Ouch.
I froze and made sure not to make eye contact. I felt a rush of heat take over my body. My heart felt as if it had fallen to the floor—crushed to a million pieces. I felt so embarrassed and ashamed. Nonetheless, I completely pretended not to hear a word. From that day forward, I even began using shyness as a defense

mechanism by pretending not to hear people. Selective "hearing" was my coping device, further giving me an excuse not to speak. I was so hurt that day that my morale had sunk to a new low. I thought my gradual progress had been paying off— then this! What made matters worse, was being in awkward situations when I had to complete class projects with them, and I would know they were only feigning kindness. I wondered who else had been pretending to like me. I felt inadequate, insecure and abnormal—yet again. I lost trust in people and assumed everyone around me felt the same about me. I was devastated and scarred for a very long time…but I didn't stay in that place.

On many occasions, I would rehearse talking in the mirror at home all by myself—I would dramatize the times someone emotionally assaulted me, and I'd confront them. I would question their motives, as if I was interviewing them. It would go something like this:
Me: "Why are you so mean to me?"
Them: "Because I hate you"
Me: "I don't hate you. We could be such good friends if you would only stop being mean to me. I care about you".

This had become a method of release for me and I found I didn't harbour resentment or even anger towards the very people that inflicted pain on me. I believe this had a lot to do with my Christian upbringing. It truly gave me a sense of release. I forgave fast and with time, I learned to let go of the pain.

Luke 23:34
"Then said Jesus, Father, forgive them; for they know not what they do…"

Matthew 5:44
"But I say unto you, love your enemies, bless them that curse you, do good to them that hate you, and pray for them which despitefully use you, and persecute you"

Chapter 7

Church Life

One of the places where I felt comfortable and unrestrained by the grip of Selective Mutism over time was Church. I was an active participant in Sunday school and had even joined Pioneer Clubs, where the message of the gospel was integrated into fun arts and crafts. I enjoyed it immensely. I even recited memory verses in front of the congregation on a weekly basis—solo! Later on, I began to play the flute during the church service and volunteered in the nursery since I loved children and they had a natural affinity to me. This was one of the social settings in which I felt safe, happy and free.

OUT AND ABOUT

When I was out in public settings with my family, I behaved normally but became very self-conscious and shy the moment I noticed someone looking at me. If someone tried to talk to me, I'd become very awkward, and usually hide behind my mom and bite the skin around my fingers. The most response I would relinquish would be a half-bitten smile.

SET APART

In addition to having a severe anxiety disorder, there were things that set me apart from my peers due to my cultural, traditional and religious upbringing.

Being that I am Italian and attended a public school, I was already a minority. My mom would pack me a very nutritiously colourful authentic Italian meal. This was not the status quo at school (typically a P&B and Jelly sandwich); therefore, I was often picked on for eating a "different" lunch. God forbid the short, olive-skinned, long brown-haired shy girl brought a provolone cheese, arugula, prosciutto and salami panino to school—with a banana, an orange and a juice thermos! (Yeah, perhaps a little much.) To add insult to injury, I already had a major complex about eating in public. This enhanced my anxiety. I thought I had solved the problem when I began to secretly throw out my lunches, until I was caught by my lunchroom supervisor one day. She was very gracious with me and promised not to get me in trouble with my parents if I promised never to do it again, to which I hesitantly obliged.

Due to my Christian beliefs, I didn't celebrate Hallowe'en and skipped school on the 31st of October. When the class worked on Hallowe'en projects leading up to the day, I sat it out and worked on a different activity.

I also didn't believe in Santa, so I quietly (of course) listened to my peers rave about the gifts he brought them. Of course, my parents told me where the gifts really came from, so this didn't bother me. I felt I had an advantage since I knew something they didn't. Fortunately for them, due to my still tongue, the secret didn't escape!

CHAPTER 8

SENSORY PROCESSING ISSUES

Due to lack of information on SM, it is hard to fully understand the symptoms I experienced, let alone describe them. It is known that other neurological disorders can overlap, be masked by or even be misdiagnosed in those with SM, such as Sensory Processing Disorder, Autism, ADHD and many others.

SMALL APPETITE

My mom recounts that since I was born, I had a very small appetite. The doctor chalked it up as me having a very small stomach.

This was difficult for my Italian mother who took so much pride in feeding her children. I ate so little, she had to resort to giving me cereal biscuits crushed in milk as a main staple. I enjoyed this beverage so much that I indulged in it well past toddlerhood. It had to be prepared in a very specific way; in a baby bottle, with the small whole cut at the top to allow the thick chunks to be slurped through.

As I got older, I remember not being able to eat very much and getting full very quickly until my stomach would hurt. I would lie down on my stomach everyday after dinner until the pain would subside. This continued until my mid-teens.

PICKY

I had a strong aversion to certain foods and textures. Just the smell of bananas made me gag. I was turned off by yogurt (especially the fruit chunk variety), cheese and plain white milk. I was absolutely disgusted by tomato sauce that had seeds in it. The sauce in itself was delicious, but when I bit on a seed I immediately wanted to throw up. In my adolescence, those aversions went away, and my appetite grew—and how!

TEXTURE

I hated certain fabrics, such as wool and corduroy. I absolutely cringed at wearing wool leggings and wanted to tear them off. Long sleeve shirts, sweaters and turtle- necks really irritated me. I always pulled my sleeves up because I couldn't stand the feeling of the fabric touching my arms.

I did not enjoy having my hair done in braids or pigtails—no matter how cute it made me look. Throughout the day, they would feel so tight my head would hurt.

VISUAL ANOMALY

A very bizarre thing I experienced probably until I was about seven or eight years old was what I can only describe as a cross between claustrophobia and some kind of an ocular perception malfunction; when someone would be speaking to me, they seemed to enlarge and move closer towards me, similar to when you zoom in on a picture on your smartphone. It was very strange but not scary. It didn't necessarily happen when I was in 'mute mode'. I remember feeling like I had to move back and telling my mom she was getting really "close" and "big". I don't think she understood what I was experiencing.

HOT FLASHES

I recall sitting in class and getting awful hot flashes—as far back as my elementary school years. This would occur randomly, without having been put on the spot. I was also hot in general. I couldn't bear the feeling of long sleeves to begin with. I stopped feeling these hot flashes well into my teens, only to later experience them during pregnancy—you can't win them all!

OVERWHELMED

My heart would begin to pound, and my stomach would flutter when the doorbell rang. A mix of excitement and nervousness would overwhelm me. I looked forward to company but had this strange anxiety that I could not explain when I was expecting them. It puzzled me.

"STIMMING" BEHAVIOURS

Self-stimulatory behaviours are also common in people with neurological disorders.

ROCKING

A strange repetitive phenomenon was that I rocked back and forth on the couch and bounced my head on the pillow in bed to put myself asleep. I couldn't sit still. I felt as though the movement was comforting and relaxing. I would often play loud music, sometimes through my headphones and just rock for the duration of an entire CD. I remember doing this from as far back as I can remember until I was in my 'tweens'.

LEG SHAKING

I would often shake my leg up and down without even being aware I was doing it. People would ask me if I was nervous or had to use the bathroom—ironically, those were the times I was most relaxed. It continues to this day, but I am more aware of my body and can control it.

FINGER BITING

I bit the skin around my fingers so often they looked like wrinkled prunes. I still have this tendency.

Many of the symptoms I described were not brought to anyone's attention simply because I had chalked it up to them being normal. I didn't know any different and grew accustomed to them.

CHAPTER 9

GROWING PAINS

Despite the disadvantages and constant attacks I faced on a routine basis, the things that kept me grounded and helped me persevere were the love, strength and unconditional support I received from my mother in particular. The other undeniable factor was my faith in God and the confidence in my own abilities that was always inculcated in me since as far back as I could remember. I firmly believe that this was the building block to my progressive recovery. It's what has made who I am today. That spark that lied deep down within me was what boosted my confidence as I got older and propelled me to build new friendships and strengthen existing ones.

The strength that grew in me allowed me to see things in a different light, and this social progression aided me in supporting my younger brother who would eventually follow in mine and my older brother's footsteps later on.

By this time, the elementary school we all attended had become relatively familiar with Selective Mutism (still known as Elective Mutism at the time) upon receiving recent back-to-back experience and information, thanks to big brother and I. The school had devised a program to monitor my younger brother's academic progress, which involved selecting me as an intermediary aid in delivering his education.

Basically, this involved a regime where I would be daily pulled out of classes for a period of time, to be taken into a private room to then spend time alone with my brother (who felt completely comfortable and open with me) and encouraged him to talk through his school work, as his voice was being recorded on a cassette. This system allowed for teachers to review his work in order to academically evaluate him. Throughout the next couple of years, I relived my past through my younger brother as I watched him endure the same strife, I had endured just a few years before. To this day, I am grateful that due to our closeness in age, I had the opportunity to support him academically and in difficult social situations. We hung out a lot in and outside of the school setting and had developed a strong bond.

I feel that the experiences I endured with SM, forced me to mature prematurely, which consequently allowed me to develop a very distinct and clear understanding of right and wrong at a very early age. As I progressed socially and felt more comfortable communicating with other children, despite still being very shy and withdrawn in public, I was particularly drawn to making friendships with children who were also social outcasts or discriminated against. I felt that sticking to what I believed in built the strength and confidence within me that would pave the way to a promisingly brighter future, free from the oppression of social anxiety.

CHAPTER 10

MULTIPLE PERSONALITIES?

When I was on my turf, I was a different child—this was before and after I showed signs of Selective Mutism. I was the leader on my block. I went to friends' doors to call on them to play. I would gather kids and organize games together. We would ride our bikes all around the block, screaming all the way down the bumpy sloped road. You read that correctly, I would scream. We would break-up into teams and build forts in the nearby woods. We climbed trees. There were three pear trees and a large pussy willow tree in my backyard—I loved climbing them to pick fruit and decorative branches for my mom. We built snowmen and igloos in the winter and had 'tea' parties inside. We tobogganed daily down the steep hill in the back field. I organized make-over parties where I would style my friends' hair, do their make-up and paint their nails. I even came up with my own perfume recipe, at the expense of my mother's beautiful red rose garden. Soccer was a passion of mine, although most of the girls weren't interested. I had gained a reputation for being "tough" and "skilled" for a girl. I knew how to kick a ball and won every arm wrestling match—even with the boys. I didn't look like a tom-boy, nor did I consider myself one, but ironically enough I had this incredible ability to adapt to different environments when I was in my comfort zone. I was quite versatile in my interests—I absolutely loved cosmetics, fashion and anything in the arts.

When I was on my turf, I exhibited a rich and colourful spectrum of hobbies and passions—out loud. If only I was able to express myself the same way at school...

PERSONALITY NUMBER TWO

At school—I went catatonic. My only method of expression was through art. I was in my element when I was in art class or music. Drawing was one of my strong points and was always recognized for being the most skilled artist by teachers and classmates alike. Music was another outlet for me. When I entered the sixth grade, I discovered another great passion that I would later pursue with excellence throughout high school—playing the flute. It allowed me to express myself in an unrestricted way. It gave me so much freedom, joy and satisfaction. It was a language all on its own, and often conveyed what I couldn't through speech.

CHAPTER 11
Middle School: 1992-1995

MILESTONES

It was more prominently in middle school that I started to feel more comfortable in my own skin and open about my sense of humor. It was then when I realized that I was actually liked by people, which encouraged me to speak up and realize that I had nothing to be afraid of in the institutional setting.

As I grew more confident, I began to express a rather eclectic sense of style. Ironically, I never liked blending in with others. I developed my own unique look; it was never extreme, yet always had its

own flair. It was yet another thing that gave me a greater sense of individuality and authenticity.

Despite the barrage of disadvantages that came along with having Selective Mutism, I can honestly say that it did come with a blessing in disguise—at least that's how I choose to see it. The fact that I had spent so much time being introverted, heightened my sense of focus which I believe led me to achieving good grades. My introspection aided me in discovering and developing my talents, which in my case happened to be writing and the arts. I found that this was encouraging and a major confidence booster. Some great advantages which also aided in my recovery were that my peers often came to me for academic and artistic insight for projects. I also found that group-work was very productive and helpful, and served as baby steps to taking the initiative to speak to people. What I believe was the best thing I did that triggered the biggest breakthrough for me personally, was joining a band. Music and playing the flute was a very big passion of mine, and I found that joining a group of other like-minded people allowed me to overcome my fears and anxiety. I had found a place of belonging. Not only that, but performing in a band in front of a large crowd of people, while still being in a team setting was very reassuring and allowed for me to gradually overcome 'stage fright', in all senses of the word. It gave me the opportunity to shine, yet at the same time, not being singled out in the spotlight.

'Complex' Situations

One characteristic which is predominant in people suffering from SM, is the vast number of unexplained complexes. These began in my prepubescent years. In my case, I didn't want to show my toes; I first noticed this when my Phys-Ed class took a trip to the pool.

I also didn't like to eat in front of people; however, this was presumably because I was the lonely girl in the corner who didn't speak, and it made me feel self- conscious. I can recall the time I went to my best friend's house and although I was comfortable speaking around her, this was very limited and next to nil in the presence of her family members. I remember her mom had offered me an ice-cream cone and as badly as I wanted it, I became paralyzed with embarrassment and the complex of eating in public and I shut down. After a repetitive attempt to get an answer from me, she gave me a long, serious stare and then said "Well, I guess Daniela doesn't want ice cream then" and offered it to her son instead. The act alone humiliated me, and at the same time made me feel angry and frustrated at myself for acting in such an unresponsive way.

I abhorred getting attention from groups of people. Even as I was getting older, if I was in front of the class, I'd feel like I looked and sounded ridiculous to people. My complexes would grow to hyperbolic proportions; I felt as though my facial features would morph— like my Pinocchio nose and my funny looking ears. I liked keeping my ears covered, so my hair was usually down. Despite the fact that I had an amazing mother who reminded me each day of how beautiful I was inside and out—and how much God loves me—I still struggled. I knew the truth deep within, but it was as if it would get hijacked by the Lie Monster in my head the moment I entered the public domain.

Eye contact was another anomaly. I remember always evading peoples' eyes and fluttering my glance elsewhere. It wasn't until one clear summer day in grade six, when a curious friend of mine asked me "Why don't you ever look at me in the eyes when we talk?"

I couldn't answer the question. "I don't know" was all I was able to muster. I became conscious of how awkward it was. It was as if I had used reverse psychology on myself—and it worked. The complex of not eye-balling people superseded my original complex—so I challenged myself to make eye contact when speaking to people from that day forward.

CHAPTER 12

High School: 1995-1999

GETTING GROUNDED

Starting high school marked a new chapter in my life. I had turned yet another leaf and shed another layer of my old self into the past. I embraced this new milestone as an opportunity to really rediscover myself as well as allow others to see me at a deeper level. The new environment and different faces spurred me to show my true colors without the inhibitions of my former identity.

My passion for music blossomed, and I began playing with the band for large groups of people on stage, as well as participating in school competitions and taking part in winning 'Best School in the Region' on several occasions. It really shifted my perception of literally and metaphorically being in the 'spotlight'. From that moment on, I made a point of challenging my fears head on, by taking it one step at a time. I even joined choir. I enjoyed singing very much (still do) so long as it was in a group setting—or in the shower, when home alone!

I found myself setting small goals, such as simply volunteering my answers more in class, or being the first to initiate a conversation. This approach opened the door to conquering my anxieties in little gradual steps, to the point where I weaned myself out of my old way of reasoning, without even being conscious of it. Each small victory served as a fear-buster and encouraged me to move forward.

I began to feel more like a unique individual, rather than a freak of nature. I delved deeper into the things that truly define my character, such as writing and poetry. I excelled in whatever I put my mind to and did it whole-heartedly.

Ironically enough, despite my complex with speech, I was fascinated with languages and decided to pursue learning them. I brushed up on my Italian, and learned a fair amount of Spanish, and conversational French—via online chat rooms. I communicated with people who were also bilingual— we helped each other reciprocally to learn as I also met a lot of wonderful people in the process.

In my second year of high school, I had the opportunity of merging two of the things I loved: children and language. Teaching was something I was strongly considering as a career choice for the future, so I decided to do my co-op hours (volunteer hours) at an elementary school in the speech and language department. I was assigned to work with children who had speech and pronunciation problems. I found it rewarding to help children overcome their challenges, and in the process, discovered yet another hidden talent planted within me; I even exceeded my expectations with the program and succeeded in helping multiple children reach breakthroughs with their speech within a short period of time. The teachers evaluating my work were overly impressed and even took notes on what techniques I had used.

During this period in my life, I really began to acknowledge that my anxiety problem had a lot to do with my own perception of life, and not actuality. Anxiety had created big monstrous lies in my mind; they belittled me constantly:

"You can't speak"

"You would sound ridiculous"

"Nobody cares what you have to say"

"Your voice is weird"

"You're not like everyone else, you're a freak"

"You are going to be this way forever; you may as well accept it"

"You can't change now; everyone already knows you for who you are"

"Not speaking defines you."

I had the epiphany that I had been my worst enemy all along. Every time I took the initiative to prove those lies wrong, my self-esteem went up a notch. I began understanding my true worth, especially as a child of The Most High. I firmly believe that my relationship with Christ was what really kept me in the most dark and difficult times.

Those moments when I felt the most alone were the times I could almost tangibly feel God's arms around me, and His soft whisper of love and reassurance. He patiently stood by me through it all and taught me so much throughout my silent journey.

Philippians 4:13

"I can do all things through Christ which strengtheneth me."

Ephesians 2:10

"For we are his workmanship, created in Christ Jesus unto good works, which God hath before ordained that we should walk in them."

Philippians 1:6

"Being confident of this very thing, that he which hath begun a good work in you will perform it until the day of Jesus Christ"

Chapter 13

ADULTHOOD: BLOSSOMING

After graduating from high school with honors (also a booster) I followed one of my deepest artistic passions and explored the world of cosmetics—I became a makeup artist and an esthetician. Following this inclination contributed to my development on a two-tier dynamic. I was forced to deal with people on the front lines; I was very gifted with my skills, and therefore, receiving the very positive feedback from clients just bolstered my self confidence that much more.

Sometime afterwards, I felt that it was time for a change, so I returned to my studies and began a career in the medical field. This likewise continuously pushed me to work at the front lines with people and allowed me to develop social skills that I would not even have imagined. I developed the thick skin I didn't know was possible, after so many years of being a doormat.

I became the loudest and biggest joker in the workplace and radiated that to my co-workers and patients. To this day, people I'm surrounded by who didn't know me growing up, have a very hard time believing that I was ever shy, let alone a Selective Mute. Knowing that I am of worth, helping and serving the community has made me a whole different person, and has allowed me to develop emotionally and psychologically.

Today's Prognosis

I have learned so much throughout my journey and am an avid believer in life-long learning. I believe every difficulty in life can be used for good. The enemy comes with his evil devices, and God turns it around in your favour.

Genesis 50:20

"But as for you, ye thought evil against me; but God meant it unto good, to bring to pass, as it is this day, to save much people alive."

Through tribulations also come wisdom, perseverance, strength, endurance and faith.

Despite having suffered through the devastation of a failed marriage, today I am happily married with three children whom I adore and share a very special bond with. My husband Cassidy is the most extraverted, outspoken, passionate and bold person I have ever met—his presence alone encourages me to live unapologetically courageous. He is also a singer/songwriter who has always been comfortable performing in front of large audiences. This has truly encouraged me to come out of my shell.

My most recent career switch is—stay-at-home-mom, and I plan to homeschool my two little ones. I am still in awe of how God works things out at the least expected time and in the least expected of ways! He is good! I also take the time (in between naps and bedtimes) to blog about my life experiences and write poetry and books. I am deeply enthralled by research in various areas of life—the Bible, social and political issues, health and nutrition, parenting styles and techniques and the list continues. I have a great passion for learning and helping others through my own learning and experiences. In 2018, my husband and I co-released a relationship book entitled "What Love Is Not"—which led us to start up a healing marriage ministry together, called MAKE YOUR MARRIAGE GREAT AGAIN. You can find out more about our ministry at www.MakeYourMarriageGreatAgain.ca.

Who would have ever known?!

We host marriage conferences where we—get this—SPEAK—PUBLICALLY—and use our platform to share our story of redemption from our failed marriage histories. God is good! Never, in a million years, would I ever have imagined that this awkward, weird, class freak mute would one day SPEAK in front of large crowds of people.

The Struggles: Anxiety

As blessed as I consider myself in overcoming Selective Mutism, I find myself still struggling with some aspects of anxiety. Socially, I still find myself getting awkward in some settings. I could be having a one-on-one conversation and be totally comfortable or begin to go blank and stumble on my words. This can happen in group settings as well. It can be frustrating, but I try not to dwell on it and simply focus on doing better the next time.

I have also become more meticulous with age—perhaps a little much. I jokingly still throw around the word "OCD" when talking to friends. I often find myself wanting to have things done a certain way and in a certain order. I also get overwhelmed at the thought of too many tasks ahead or simply too many ideas at once. I am still learning to become more aware of this feeling and to just step back and breathe. Breaking down tasks and spreading them out makes life easier. I find myself putting a lot of pressure on myself for getting things done, and often feel disappointed in myself if I cannot follow through. I often have to remind myself that it isn't the end of the world if I can't meet every single imaginary deadline on my list. (I run a tight ship!)

Having babies has made me recognize how anxious I get when they cry. There are times I literally feel frozen with anxiety and cannot focus on any other task until the crying stops. I especially experienced this when I was sleep training my babies and the crying escalated more than usual. My husband would tell me to just do something else and take my focus away from the crying, but I literally could not. Nonetheless, I persisted.

I also have struggled a lot with intimacy and sharing deeply personal things about myself, especially expressing emotions. In situations where people would be expected to cry, I hold it in. It takes a lot for me to share painful experiences with people and have often kept it to myself. It is only in recent years that I have been comfortable opening up (in my thirties). I give my husband a lot of credit for this!

I've also developed some unexplainable phobias over the years: the fear of flying, cars driving too close, spinning rides (that I used to love) and small spaces, which I discovered while having an MRI.

One scripture I meditate on frequently is 2 Corinthians 10:5

"Casting down imaginations, and every high thing that exalteth itself against the knowledge of God, and bringing into captivity every thought to the obedience of Christ"

This scripture keeps me grounded and serves as a great reminder that feelings and perceptions are not rooted in truth. I find much encouragement in knowing that things don't have to remain stuck in the prison of my mind. I am indeed a work in progress.

SENSORY PROCESSING ISSUES

- I am very easily startled; someone can just walk up behind me or start talking and I'll jump

- I'm a little clumsy; I drop things and bump into things quite frequently

- Loud sounds, music or bright lights can make me irritable; they trigger headaches and lack of focus

- Many types of fragrances trigger immediate headaches and even migraines

- I feel like the world around me goes into 'slow motion' on occasion when feeling overwhelmed

- Being in crowded spaces or parties overwhelms me, especially if I am the host—I playfully dub it 'ADHD'

- Over-excitement sometimes triggers and instant headache and my right leg to throb

- Hats, scarves (especially wool), long sleeves, or anything around my neck, as well as certain jewelry irritate me

- High ponytails hurt after a short time, especially when tight they trigger headaches

- Random scalp tenderness

- Wearing contact lenses and glasses cause me headaches after a short time

- 'Sensory "overload' when there is too much noise, clutter, or too many people around mainly at night. Sometimes when I am talking with someone my eyes begin to feel "dizzy" and my mind feels like it is racing. It gets hard to focus, especially if they are loud, make too many body gestures, speak too fast or get too close into my personal space. I have to actually look down or away from them, step back and take deep breaths.

- Get cold and hot very quickly as well as hot flashes; when I get too hot, I feel nauseated, clammy, irritable and as if blacking out at times.

- I find myself being tense especially in my upper back and neck— I make a conscious effort to relax when I notice it.

"STIMS"

I feel as though I constantly need to be stimulated, either physically or mentally. I have a hard time just relaxing or vegetating. This is probably why I love research, reading and writing so much. It is a release for me.

When I am reading, especially something I am engrossed in I begin to pick at the skin of my nails. You can usually tell I've been reading a great book by looking at my fingers!

Chapter 14

Confidence Tips

It is so important for SM sufferers to find activities in their comfort zones, but within a group setting. Even if it is only with very few limited people that person speaks around or feels at ease with. In fact, according to my parents, the biggest breakthrough for all three of us always came after the summer vacation. I am convinced that a huge component of our recovery was due to the large amount of social exposure in our familiar surroundings during the summer months.

I encourage pursuing any activity that establishes a sense of accomplishment and conquers fear- i.e. Swimming, skiing, skating, roller-coaster riding, etc. and if age appropriate, even skydiving or zip-lining water skiing etc. I recommend this incentive for anybody at any stage of life who struggles with SM. Parents—the younger you involve your children in these activities the better the outcome will probably be. Exploring these new boundaries awakens in you a strength that you never knew you had and will help you establish a solid sense of self-worth, which will in turn aid you to conquer your fear of speaking.

Animals always held a special place in my heart from a young age. My parents succumbed to my desires on various occasions and welcomed many pets in our home over the years; from turtles to birds to cats, to dogs. These creatures always had a way of calming me and filling me with instant joy. If your child suffers from Selective Mutism and adores animals, try using this as a creative avenue to not only alleviate anxiety, but to make opportunities for connecting with other like-minded children.

As an outlet, I take pleasure in artistic activities such as reading, poetry, blogging, book writing, playing the flute, fooling around on the keyboard and drawing. I strongly encourage taking part in activities that not only are a personal passion but are two-tiered and serve as a way to help others. I found that this dramatically increased my confidence and it is unfathomably rewarding.

STAY POSITIVE

Over time, what I found to be the most impactful thing I've ever understood is the power of positive thinking. I can't stress enough how important it is to eliminate negative thoughts and replace them with good ones. As a former child with Selective Mutism, I can attest to the fact that life with this anxiety disorder is no box of chocolates. It is very easy to become negative or bitter, or even fall into a deep depression. This is precisely why a positive thinking lifestyle is essential in overcoming these barriers and reaching out to a free and brighter future.

Rest assured that there is a spiritual factor at play in SM. It was my identity in Christ that truly challenged me to break free from my comfort zone, which was really a padded jail cell. Selective Mutism at the core really comes down to an identity issue; it is the strong belief in our inability to speak that keeps us mute. It is our perpetual belief in this false perception that keeps us from progressing. The more I became aware of this, the more I overcame. I was giving anxiety a foothold over my life, simply by coddling the idea that SM was my identity.

The important thing I'd like to emphasize on is what is known in the New Age movement as the 'law of attraction'. It states that you can actually attract positive situations and circumstances in your life by simply putting your intention and desire into thought form. There is nothing new about this concept, and there is definitely truth in it— the Bible confirms it.

Proverbs 18:21

"Death and life are in the power of the tongue: and they that love it shall eat the fruit thereof."

Philippians 4:8

"Finally, brethren, whatsoever things are true, whatsoever things are honest, whatsoever things are just, whatsoever things are pure, whatsoever things are lovely, whatsoever things are of good report; if there be any virtue, and if there be any praise, think on these things."

Proverbs 17:22

"A merry heart doeth good like a medicine: but a broken spirit drieth the bones."

It is important to note that just as positive thinking brings about good results, the opposite is likewise true and proven by the very existence of Selective Mutism disorder. The Biblical standard is replete with effective methods of dealing with all different life situations and circumstances. It is a roadmap to life which is relevant and transcends the barriers of time and cultural diversity. Having said this, thoughts of fear and constant negativity actually have the proven ability to paralyze one's speech.

I can't stress enough that you practice positive thinking and apply it to every area of life. This is a step by step process. It is important to remember, however, that progress doesn't happen overnight. Any achievement of worth is not easily acquired. I would highly recommend joining a child to a church youth group or Bible study at a young age. The teaching of sound Biblical principles combined with the unity of other youth, and the guidance as well as dependability of a leader (including the availability of one-on-one support) can prove extremely beneficial for a child's well-being. We must not forget that we are not only physical beings, but spiritual ones as well—the two cannot be separated.

AFFIRMING SCRIPTURES

My Christian upbringing truly played a large role in paving the way to my recovery. The fact that Jesus calls me His own and promises soundness of mind gave me boldness. Our belief system has an incredible impact on our body and mind. How much more would my identity as a princess of the King of kings have an impact? Reading the Word of God fueled a great sense of uniqueness and purpose within me. I simply couldn't stay in that prison cell of silent doom forever. God gave me reassurance through the Bible—His Word, and prayer, and I decided in my mind that I would overcome.

There is a spiritual component behind muteness and anxiety: This is confirmed in scripture. It is a tormenting spirit, and I believe I speak for the entire SM community when I say that living with Selective Mutism can be absolute torment. It is as if something outside of yourself is literally paralyzing and choking your voice.

Mark 9:25

"Running together, he rebuked the foul spirit, saying unto him, thou dumb and deaf spirit, I charge thee, come out of him, and enter no more into him."

FEAR AND ANXIETY

2 Timothy 1:7

"For God hath not given us the spirit of fear; but of power, and of love, and of a sound mind."

It is important to inject truth into our minds if we are to overcome darkness. Jesus is the way, the truth and the life. This is why I firmly believe that speaking scriptures as often as possible over yourself, or your child(ren) with SM is essential in defeating this debilitating disorder. God is the Great Physician, and His Word brings life, healing and peace.

John 1:12

"But as many as received him, to them gave he power to become the sons of God, even to them that believe on his name"

Colossians 2:10

"And ye are complete in him, which is the head of all principality and power"

Ephesians 3:12

"In whom we have boldness and access with confidence by the faith of him."

Take The Bull By The Horns

Remember to set small challenges for yourself in overcoming your fears—don't start too big otherwise it might backfire and create a bigger phobia than what you started with. This advice applies to those who still struggle SM and those who have progressed but still struggle with anxiety.

For instance, if you normally like to stay in the shadows; how about joining a creative extracurricular activity? Even if you aren't ready to come out of your 'voice box' yet, just the act of participating in an activity that you love will ease your anxiety, boost your self-confidence and reduce your feelings of inferiority.

When setting goals, if I know it will cause me anxiety, I make sure to give myself a small time frame to get it done. Too much time allows for procrastination and creates opportunities to cop out.

For example, if I had planned to speak to someone about an uncomfortable issue or attend an interview, I push myself to do it quickly. I find this doesn't give me time to stew over it and obsess over how nervous I will be and find an excuse to change my mind. I will probably lose sleep over it—which is an additional motivator to get it done quickly!

Chapter 15

Say No to Pharmaceutical Drugs

I'm on controversial grounds, but my conviction on this topic is so strong that I decided to take the plunge and talk about it anyways. I will add the disclaimer that I am not a medical doctor or professional. I base my belief on personal research, which has led me to the conclusion that the least medical intervention is always best. I believe this applies to all areas of life. I am convinced that pharmaceuticals may provide temporary relief, but in the long term, they are debilitating—and I'll explain why; there are always repercussions to drugs. They are toxins and not only have harmful potential side effects, but cause long term dependency as well. This is like creating a more comfortable prison cell. You never plan on leaving, so you may as well make it as cushy as possible. It is further enabling the problem, because rather than getting to the root, we just suppress it. See the problem? Why not escape the prison cell? In my humble opinion, the only way to face and tackle anxiety is head on, and in gradual steps, naturally.

As a result of my passion for research and healthy living, I have come to learn many new things in my adult years. I believe these natural approaches can truly help someone suffering with SM, regardless of their age. Firstly, as I mentioned above, I have never used pharmaceutical drugs for my condition and truly believe I would have been in a worse place had I done so. I have used natural approaches, however, to literally cure myself of many ailments such as acid reflux. I am a strong believer that our Creator has provided us with every fruit, herb, root and plant for our healing.

Revelation 22:2 is one of many scriptures revealing this:

"In the midst of the street of it, and on either side of the river, was there the tree of life, which bare twelve manner of fruits, and yielded her fruit every month: and the leaves of the tree were for the healing of the nations."

Let's take a look at how gut health is important for the brain. In recent studies, a link has been found between gut and neurological issues;

According to an article written in Science Daily on May 29, 2016 by the European Academy of Neurology entitled: "Connections between gut microbiota and the brain":

"Intestinal bacteria that can boost bravery or trigger multiple sclerosis: An increasing body of research results confirms the importance of the "gut-brain axis" for neurology and indicates that the triggers for a number of neurological diseases may be located in the digestive tract."

DIETARY TIPS

- Change your diet to include as much raw organic food as possible, and eliminate sugars and processed foods

- Consider eliminating gluten

- Add Prebiotics and Probiotics to your diet

- The use of essential oils goes as far back as ancient times. Consider the gifts the wise men gave to baby Jesus; Frankincense and Myrrh were among them.

Essential oils for diffusion are very safe and effective for just about any ailment. Copaiba, Frankincense and Lavender together are excellent for supporting the neurological system and easing anxiety and are generally safe for all ages.

- Consider seeing a naturopath/holistic practitioner for herbal remedies

CHAPTER 16

LIGHT AT THE END OF THE TUNNEL

As can be summarized, my struggle with SM was not easy and short lived. I went through diverse stages as I reached different levels of maturity, and finally reached a pinnacle that marked a turning point in my life. I spent a lot of time reflecting on my life and realized there were things I wanted to change and simply refused to live with. In order to come to terms with my decision, I was going to have to accept the challenge to take an active role in changing the way I responded to certain situations. I realized that nobody was going to do this for me but me. I wanted so much to be like everyone else, yet to them, it came so naturally. For me, the simple idea of attempting to talk and laugh comfortably in public was a nightmare. I had to come to terms with the fact that the way I was responding to the world around me was not normal, and that if I started to condition myself to behave like my true self, it would be OK. In fact, as I put this theory to the test, I quickly learned that it was more than OK. It was during this time that my prayer life really took off. My faith in God gave me the confidence and knowledge that I was never alone—God was always there with me through my struggles, and when I reached a point where I was scared beyond my capacity, He was there to comfort and reassure me.

I started to set small goals to gradually open myself up to the rest of the world. The following examples of such goals helped me tremendously and have proven to help me overcome a severe myriad of complexes. I recommend giving these techniques a try:

- Challenge yourself to be the first to say hi or simply wave at someone

- If the teacher/professor asks the class a question and you know the answer, put up your hand—start off by answering 'yes' or 'no' questions, then as you feel more comfortable, answer more elaborate questions

- When a new friend or acquaintance shares a story with you, relate by sharing a similar scenario or simply provide feedback on their story, even if it's short

- If you're accustomed to always wearing a certain style or colors, change it up a bit by trying something different—I'm not suggesting a complete overhaul, but a little tweak will automatically be noticed and is usually followed by positive feedback, which will help break you out of your 'label' or 'mold', boost your self-confidence and give you boldness to do other things you don't normally do

- If you have friends you are comfortable speaking around, challenge yourself to introduce them to each other. Get together, laugh, take part in a fun activity and share stories

- Try to plan things in a public setting. If you have friends you normally hang out with in private, take it to the next level by going out to a game/church group/movie. The idea is to take it out of your comfort zone. Just being around other people has a very refreshing effect on your social skills—and you never know who you'll encounter. This opens up the doors to new opportunities to meet new people, and will snowball into self-improvement

- Is there something you are very passionate about? Perhaps volunteering is a good outlet for you. This not only will allow you to interact with people and build your social skills, but in turn, will reap fulfillment in the knowledge that you are giving to the community

- Are you particularly talented or creative? Do you have a specific interest? How about joining an art class? Pottery lessons? An astronomy course? A health food seminar? The sky's the limit. Grab a friend, or just go at it on your own. You'll be surprised at how comfortable you'll feel in an environment where people around you share the same passion and interests as you. Communication will flow a lot more naturally, and you'll be able to make social connections that will serve as a stepping stone for the future.

- Last but certainly not least, do as much research as possible on Selective Mutism. This goes for parents as well. In my personal experience, this has aided me in identifying the problem by name, rather than thinking I was just a freak of nature or misfit. By learning more about others like you, and about how others have overcome it, you will be reassured in the knowledge that you are not alone. It will provide you with the necessary tools to identify the characteristics of SM in order to tackle and overcome them.

Chapter 17

Embrace Your Quirks

Selective Mutism does come with a lot of baggage, but not all of it is burdensome! You are wired differently, and the more you recognize what makes you tick, the more you will overcome. You may be so focused on the overwhelming negatives that come with SM that you may overlook the wonderful things that come with the package. It is all a matter of perspective. Think about SM as a chisel and a stimulator for creativity. Reflect on how SM has made you better. Look harder. For me, I found my 'empathy-meter' was very high and it propelled me to show kindness and compassion to those who were ill- treated. I also found my outlet for expression to be in the form of writing. So, I created beautiful poetry, eventually created a blog and began writing books. I loved music, so I learned a musical instrument and joined a band. There is a richness of unique creativity locked up deep inside the well of your soul. Let it flow.

Scripture tells us that the opposite of fear is love. There is a principle in this—when you love others using your gifts and creative abilities, it conquers fear.

1 John 4:18

"There is no fear in love; but perfect love casteth out fear: because fear hath torment. He that feareth is not made perfect in love."

LOVE IS THE BEST CURE.

WHERE DO YOU GET IT?

STRAIGHT FROM THE SOURCE.

1 John 4:16

"And we have known and believed the love that God hath to us. God is love; and he that dwelleth in love dwelleth in God, and God in him."

You wield the power in yourself to do great things. Don't underestimate yourself. With God on your side, you can move mountains. Don't waste the gifts He has buried inside of you; they are meant to be used.

Selective Mutes typically have these things in common:

- Above-average intelligence, perception, or inquisitiveness
- Creativity, a strong imagination and a love for art or music
- Empathy and sensitivity to others' thoughts and feelings
- A strong sense of right and wrong
- A high level of concentration

It would be a shame to put such great potential to waste! Scriptures remind us to be good stewards of the talents we were given.

Matthew 5:14-15

"Ye are the light of the world. A city that is set on an hill cannot be hid. Neither do men light a candle, and put it under a bushel, but on a candlestick; and it giveth light unto all that are in the house."

1 Corinthians 4:2

"Moreover, it is required in stewards, that a man be found faithful."

1 Peter 4:10

"As every man hath received the gift, even so minister the same one to another, as good stewards of the manifold grace of God."

If there is one thing I hope will resonate with you it's that you have a purpose. It is my greatest desire that through sharing my experience, I will have provided some of the tools to help you—or someone you know, in overcoming Selective Mutism. My utmost objective in writing this book was precisely and exclusively for the purpose of edifying and motivating you to unlock the rich potential that lies within you. I pray that this book will make a positive impact in someone's life, in defeating the silence.

ABOUT THE AUTHOR

DANIELA PARLANE is married to Cassidy Parlane, and is a Relationship Coach, Podcaster, an avid blogger, a co-author with her husband, of the book "What Love Is Not" and a home-schooling mom of three. Together they have embarked on a healing marriage ministry entitled MAKE YOUR MARRIAGE GREAT AGAIN in Hamilton, Ontario, Canada. It is Daniela's passion to use her gift of writing to bring healing, hope and restoration to her readers, as she shares her most vulnerable, impactful and victorious experiences through her writing.

Learn more about Daniela at
www.MakeYourMarriageGreatAgain.ca

CHECK OUT MY OTHER BOOK

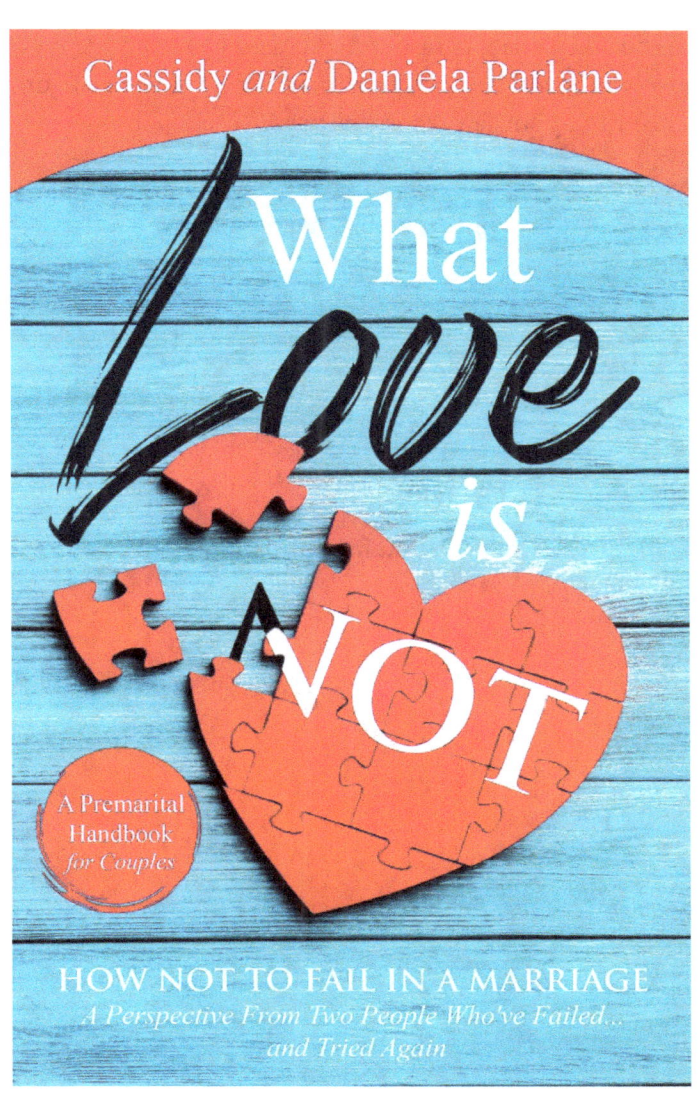

[What Love Is Not](#)

ONE LAST THING...

If you enjoyed this book or found it useful, I'd be very grateful if you'd post a short review on Amazon. Your support really does make a difference, and your feedback matters!

If you'd like to leave a review, then all you need to do is follow the review link on Amazon below:

Leave an Amazon Review

Thanks again for your support!

www.ingramcontent.com/pod-product-compliance
Lightning Source LLC
Chambersburg PA
CBHW072039080526
44578CB00007B/491